The Deliverance Topical Bible

John Eckhardt

DEDICATION

Dedicated to all of Daddy God's Children,
Deliverance is your Bread.

ACKNOWLEDGMENTS

I want to thank Prophet Lauro Adame for helping
me compile this Topical Bible.

INTRODUCTION

There are numerous scriptures on deliverance. The large number shows us the importance deliverance is given in the Word of God. This Topical Bible is a handy reference tool for those who desire to meditate and familiarize themselves with the subject of deliverance.

The following list of Greek and Hebrew words that are part of the lexicon of the ministry of deliverance.

The Greek word EKBALLO (Mark 16:17) means to cast out, drive out, expel, eject. Casting out demons (ekballo) is a sign that follows believers. Jesus cast out many devils (Mark 1:34), and cast evils out of many (Luke 4:41). His disciples also cast out many devils (Mark 6:13).

The word SALVATION also means deliverance, freedom, and healing. The LORD is our Savior and Deliverer. SAVE is the Greek word SOZO meaning to save, keep safe and sound, to rescue from danger or destruction, to save a suffering one from perishing, to heal, restore to health, to preserve one who is in danger of destruction, to save or rescue.

The Hebrew word for SAVIOR and SALVATION is the word YASHA which is used more than 100 times in the Old Testament. It means to have ample room enough to shelter and supplies enough for support after being delivered from danger. (Psalm 34:6; Isaiah 12:2; 49:26; 52;13; 53:12)

PALAT (Psalm 40:17) is the Hebrew word for DELIVERER. It means to slip away or escape. It describes the One who makes us smooth and slippery by His anointing to escape; the Lord our Great Deliverer. (Psalm 18:12)

There are two Hebrew words for DELIVER. The first is NATSAL (Psalm 22:8; 255:20) which has a few meanings. First, it means to take away or snatch away, as to take away riches and wealth. (2 Chron. 20:25) Secondly, it also means to spoil. (Exodus 3:22) Thirdly, it means to preserve and defend. (Exodus 14:14) And it also means to escape as slave would and to find refuge where there is no extradition. (Deut. 23:15,16)

The second Hebrew word for DELIVER is the word CHALATS (Proverbs 11:8). It means to be delivered or pulled out as from trouble and death. It also means to withdraw or pull out of.

The Greek word translated POSSESSED (Mark 1:32) is DAIMONIZOMAI the word meaning to be under the power of a demon, or demonized.

DAIMONIODES (James 3:15) is the Greek word for DEVILSH, DEMONIC or DIABOLICAL.

OPPRESSED (Acts 10:38) is the Greek word KATADYNASTEUO meaning to exercise harsh control over one, to use one's power against one.

VEXED (Luke 6:18) is the Greek word OCHLEO meaning to excite a mob against one, to disturb, trouble, molest, troubled by demons. Another Greek word is KATAPONEO (2 Peter 2:7) meaning to wear down, to tire down with toil, exhaust with labor; hence, to afflict or oppress with evils; to make trouble for; to treat roughly.

DAROR (Isaiah 61:1) is the Hebrew word for LIBERTY or FREEDOM. It means to flow, sparkle or radiate with the Glory of the Lord. (Isaiah 9:2) And it was Jesus Christ himself that radiated with the Glory of His Father to set the captives free and bring liberty to the bruised. (Luke 4:18; John 1:4, 5, 14) This is what Jesus meant and wanted his followers to do, to shine with the light of His Glory among the people in order to bring liberty to them and glory to the Father. (Matthew 5:14-16)

How God anointed Jesus of Nazareth with the Holy Ghost and with power: who went about doing good, and healing all that were oppressed of the devil; for God was with him.
Acts 10:38

Jesus said in John 10:7 & 9 *"I am the Door…"*
The word Door in the Hebrew is the word PETACH (Psalm 24:7) It has several meanings, but there is one definition in particular which means to let loose, to set free, like opening a "Door" to let the captives out of prison. (Isaiah 14:17) And for the Body of Christ, He is standing at the "Door" to deliverer us. (Revelation 3:17-20)

HA-SATAN (Zechariah 3:2) is the Hebrew word for SATAN which means the following: accuser, opponent, enemy, adversary, hater, slanderer.

DIABOLOS (Matthew 4:1) is Greek word for DEVIL. Which describes an adversary that is throwing fiery missiles. (Eph. 6:16) Also means enemy, persecutor, murderer, slanderer, critic, and liar. (John10:10)
MASHAL (Psalm 8:6) is the Hebrew word for DOMINION. It means to rule, reign, to have dominion, to exercise power.

DEO (Matthew 18:18) is the Greek word for BINDING. It means to legally bound, binding, or bound. There are two Hebrew words connected to this word, the first is DESMEUO (Matthew 23:4; Acts 22:4) which means to bind a heavy legal burden upon one without assistance. It also means to put one in a prison with heavy chains. The second word is DESMEO (Luke 8:29) which means chains. DEO has two uses, the first is to prohibit, to declare unlawful with imposing a legal ban or prohibition. The second used in prayer, intercession or spiritual warfare. (Matthew 12:29)

LUO (Matthew 16:19; 18:19) is the Greek word for LOOSING. It means to unloose, loosing, loose. It is used in the following legal terms, to declare lawful, allowable, to annul, to abrogate, and it also means to legally bring to an end to that which was prohibited. For the spiritual life of the believer it means, freedom, to discharge, to liberate, to undo the heavy chains or to break away from them, and it also means to set free. It makes the powers of sin, sickness and satan null and void. (Luke13:12)
Israel was told to drive out the nations from Canaan and possess the land. This was a type of Christ's ministry in driving out demons which he

commissioned his disciples to do as well. A lack of deliverance will allow the enemy to operate in the lives of believers without interference.

Deliverance is the children's bread (Matthew 15:26). Believers should receive deliverance and minister deliverance.

Common spirits people need deliverance from include rejection, rebellion, bitterness, hurt, anger, fear, lust, pride, discouragement, depression, sadness, loneliness, unforgiveness, infirmity, mind control, shame, guilt, confusion, poverty, witchcraft, and addiction. Area of demonization can include the mind, the emotions, the will, the appetite, the body, and the sexual character. Demons can indwell different areas of the body including the stomach, the chest, the back, the head, the eyes, the glands, the shoulders, and even organs of the body. Demons often come out of the breathing passage. The word for spirit is the word PNUEMA that means breath, wind or air.

THE DELIVERANCE TOPICAL BIBLE

The Book of Genesis

Genesis 14:18-20
And Melchizedek king of Salem brought forth bread and wine: and he was the priest of the most high God. And he blessed him, and said, Blessed be Abram of the most high God, possessor of heaven and earth: **And blessed be the most high God, which hath delivered thine enemies into thy hand.** And he gave him tithes of all.

Genesis 19:15
And when the morning arose, **then the angels hastened Lot**, saying, Arise, take thy wife, and thy two daughters, which are here; lest thou be consumed in the iniquity of the city.

Genesis 19:29
And it came to pass, when God destroyed the cities of the plain, that God remembered Abraham, a**nd sent Lot out of the midst of the overthrow,** when he overthrew the cities in the which Lot dwelt.

Genesis 32:11
Deliver me, I pray thee, from the hand of my brother, from the hand of Esau: for I fear him, lest he will come and smite me, and the mother with the children.

Genesis 37:21
And Reuben heard it, and he **delivered him out of their hands**; and said, Let us not kill him.

Genesis 45:7
And God sent me before you to **preserve** you a posterity in the earth, and to save your lives by a **great deliverance**.

Genesis 49:8
Judah, thou art he whom thy brethren shall praise: **thy hand shall be in the neck of thine enemies;** thy father's children shall bow down before thee.

Genesis 50:24
And Joseph said unto his brethren, I die: **and God will surely visit you, and bring you out of this land** unto the land which he sware to Abraham, to Isaac, and to Jacob.

The Book of Exodus

Exodus 1:14
And they made their lives bitter with hard bondage, in morter, and in brick, and in all manner of service in the field: all their service, wherein they made them serve, was with rigor.

Exodus 2:23
And it came to pass in process of time, that the king of Egypt died: **and the children of Israel sighed by reason of the bondage, and they cried, and their cry came up unto God by reason of the bondage.**

Exodus 3:8
And **I am come down to deliver them out of the hand of the Egyptians**, and to bring them up out of that land unto a good land and a large, unto a land flowing with milk and honey; unto the place of the Canaanites, and the Hittites, and the Amorites, and the Perizzites, and the Hivites, and the Jebusites.

Exodus 3:17
And I have said, **I will bring you up out of the affliction of Egypt** unto the land of the Canaanites, and the Hittites, and the Amorites, and the Perizzites, and the Hivites, and the

Jebusites, unto a land flowing with milk and honey.

Exodus 6:5-7
And I have also heard the groaning of the children of Israel, **whom the Egyptians keep in bondage; and I have remembered my covenant.** Wherefore say unto the children of Israel, **I am the Lord, and I will bring you out from under the burdens of the Egyptians, and I will rid you out of their bondage, and I will redeem you with a stretched out arm, and with great judgments:** And I will take **you** to me for a people, and I will be to you a God: and **ye shall know that I am the Lord your God, which bringeth you out from under the burdens of the Egyptians.**

Exodus 8:23
And I will put a **deliverance** between My people and thy people… (from the Keil & Delitzsh German Commentary Bible)

Exodus 12:22-23
And ye shall take a bunch of hyssop, and dip it in the blood that is in the bason, and strike the lintel and the two side posts with the blood that is in the bason; and none of you shall go out at the door of his house until the morning. **For the**

Lord will pass through to smite the Egyptians; and when he seeth the blood upon the lintel, and on the two side posts, the Lord will pass over the door, and will not suffer the destroyer to come in unto your houses to smite you.

Exodus 12:27
That ye shall say, **It is the sacrifice of the Lord's passover,** who passed over the houses of the children of Israel in Egypt, when he smote the Egyptians, **and delivered our houses. And the people bowed the head and worshipped.**

Exodus 14:14
The Lord shall fight for you, and ye shall hold your peace.

Exodus 14:16
But **lift thou up thy rod,** and stretch out thine hand over the sea, and divide it: **and the children of Israel shall go on dry ground through the midst of the sea.**

Exodus 14:21-23
And Moses stretched out his hand over the sea; and the Lord caused the sea to go back by a strong east wind all that night, and made the sea dry land, and the waters were

divided. And the children of Israel went into the midst of the sea upon the dry ground: and the waters were a wall unto them on their right hand, and on their left.

And the Egyptians pursued, and went in after them to the midst of the sea, even all Pharaoh's horses, his chariots, and his horsemen.

Exodus 14:26

And the Lord said unto Moses, Stretch out thine hand over the sea, that the waters may come again upon the Egyptians, upon their chariots, and upon their horsemen.

Exodus 15:1

Then sang Moses and the children of Israel this song unto the Lord, and spake, saying, **I will sing unto the Lord, for he hath triumphed gloriously: the horse and his rider hath he thrown into the sea.**

Exodus 15:4

Pharaoh's chariots and his host hath he cast into the sea: his chosen captains also are drowned in the Red sea.

Exodus 15:21

And Miriam answered them, **Sing ye to the Lord, for he hath triumphed gloriously; the**

**horse and his rider hath he thrown into the
sea.**

Exodus 18:9
And Jethro rejoiced for all the goodness which
the Lord had done to Israel, **whom he had
delivered out of the hand of the Egyptians.**

Exodus 18:10
And Jethro said, Blessed be the Lord, **who hath
delivered you** out of the hand of the Egyptians,
and out of the hand of Pharaoh, **who hath
delivered the people** from under the hand of
the Egyptians.

Exodus 22:18
Thou shalt not suffer a witch to live.

Exodus 23:28
**And I will send hornets before thee, which
shall drive out** the Hivite, the Canaanite, and the
Hittite, from before thee.

Exodus 23:29
I will not drive them out from before thee in
one year; lest the land become desolate, and the
beast of the field multiply against thee.

Exodus 23:30
By little and little **I will drive them out** from before thee, until thou be increased, and inherit the land.

Exodus 34:24
For I will cast out the nations before thee, and enlarge thy borders: neither shall any man desire thy land, when thou shalt go up to appear before the Lord thy God thrice in the year.

The Book of Leviticus

Leviticus 11:45
For I am the Lord that bringeth you up out of the land of Egypt, to be your God: ye shall therefore be holy, for I am holy.

Leviticus 17:7
And they shall **no more offer their sacrifices unto devils,** after whom they have gone a whoring. This shall be a statute for ever unto them throughout their generations.

Leviticus 18:24
Defile not ye yourselves in any of these things: for in all these the nations are defiled **which I cast out before you:**

Leviticus 20:23
And ye shall not walk in the manners of the
nation, **which I cast out before you**: for they
committed all these things, and therefore I
abhorred them.

Leviticus 25:10
And ye shall hallow the fiftieth year, **and
proclaim liberty throughout all the land unto
all the inhabitants thereof:** it shall be a jubilee
unto you; and ye shall return every man unto his
possession, and ye shall return every man unto
his family.

Leviticus 26:7
**And ye shall chase your enemies, and they
shall fall before you by the sword.**

Leviticus 26:8
And five of **you shall chase** an hundred, and an
hundred of **you shall put ten thousand to
flight**: and your enemies shall **fall before you by
the sword.**

The Book of Numbers

Numbers 21:3
And the Lord hearkened to the voice of Israel,
and **delivered up the Canaanites; and they**

utterly destroyed them and their cities: and he called the name of the place Hormah.

Numbers 33:52
Then ye shall drive out all the inhabitants of the land from before you, and destroy all their pictures, and destroy all their molten images, and quite pluck down all their high places:

Numbers 33:55
But if ye will not drive out the inhabitants of the land from before you; then it shall come to pass, that those which ye let remain of them shall be pricks in your eyes, and thorns in your sides, and shall vex you in the land wherein ye dwell.

Numbers 35:6
And among the cities which ye shall give unto the **Levites there shall be six cities for refuge**, which ye shall appoint for the manslayer, that he may flee thither: and to them ye shall add forty and two cities.

Numbers 35:11
Then ye shall appoint you cities to be cities of refuge for you; that the slayer may flee thither, which killeth any person at unawares.

Numbers 35:12
And **they shall be unto you cities for refuge from the avenger**; that the manslayer die not, until he stand before the congregation in judgment.

Numbers 35:13
And of these cities which ye shall give six cities **shall ye have for refuge**.

Numbers 35:14
Ye shall give three cities on this side Jordan, and three cities shall ye give in the land of Canaan, which shall be cities of **refuge**.

Numbers 35:15
These six cities shall be a refuge, both for the children of Israel, and for the stranger, and for the sojourner among them: that every one that killeth any person unawares may flee thither.

Numbers 35:25
And the congregation shall deliver the slayer out of the hand of the revenger of blood, **and the congregation shall restore him to the city of his refuge**, whither he was fled: and he shall abide in it unto the death of the high priest, which was anointed with the holy oil.

The Book of Deuteronomy

Deuteronomy 1:30
The Lord your God which goeth before you, **he shall fight for you, according to all that he did for you in Egypt before your eyes;**

Deuteronomy 3:22
Ye shall not fear them: **for the Lord your God he shall fight for you.**

Deuteronomy 4:38
To drive out nations from before thee greater and mightier than thou art, to bring thee in, to give thee their land for an inheritance, as it is this day.

Deuteronomy 5:6
I am the Lord thy God, **which brought thee out of the land of Egypt, from the house of bondage.**

Deuteronomy 6:19
To cast out all thine enemies from before thee, as the Lord hath spoken.

Deuteronomy 7:1
When the Lord thy God shall bring thee into the land whither thou goest to possess it, **and hath**

cast out many nations before thee, the Hittites, and the Girgashites, and the Amorites, and the Canaanites, and the Perizzites, and the Hivites, and the Jebusites, seven nations greater and mightier than thou;

Deuteronomy 7:23
But the Lord thy God **shall deliver them unto thee, and shall destroy them with a mighty destruction, until they be destroyed.**

Deuteronomy 7:24
And **he shall deliver their kings into thine hand, and thou shalt destroy their name from under heaven:** there shall no man be able to stand before thee, until thou have destroyed them.

Deuteronomy 9:4
Speak not thou in thine heart, after that **the Lord thy God hath cast them out from before thee,** saying, For my righteousness the Lord hath brought me in to possess this land: but for the wickedness of these nations the Lord doth drive them out from before thee.

Deuteronomy 15:1-2
At the end of every seven years thou shalt make a **release.**

And this is the manner of the release: Every creditor that lendeth ought unto his neighbor shall **release** it; he shall not exact it of his neighbor, or of his brother; **because it is called the Lord's release.**

Deuteronomy 15:12-14
And if thy brother, an Hebrew man, or an Hebrew woman, be sold unto thee, and serve thee six years; **then in the seventh year thou shalt let him go free from thee.** And when thou sendest him out free from thee, thou shalt not let him go away empty: Thou shalt furnish him liberally out of thy flock, and out of thy floor, and out of thy winepress: of that wherewith the Lord thy God hath blessed thee thou shalt give unto him.

Deuteronomy 18:10
There shall not be found among you any one that maketh his son or his daughter to pass through the fire, or that useth divination, or an observer of times, or an enchanter, or a witch.

Deuteronomy 18:14
For these nations, which thou shalt possess, hearkened unto observers of times, and unto diviners: **but as for thee, the Lord thy God hath not suffered thee so to do.**

Deuteronomy 20:4
For the Lord your God is he that goeth with you, **to fight for you against your enemies**, to save you.

Deuteronomy 30:3
That then the Lord thy God **will turn thy captivity, and have compassion upon thee, and will return and gather thee from all the nations**, whither the Lord thy God hath scattered thee.

Deuteronomy 32:17
They sacrificed unto devils, not to God; to gods whom they knew not, to new gods that came newly up, whom your fathers feared not.

Deuteronomy 32:30
How should one chase a thousand, and two put ten thousand to flight, except their Rock had sold them, and the Lord had shut them up?

The Book of Joshua

Joshua 2:24
And they said unto Joshua, **Truly the Lord hath delivered into our hands all the land;** for even all the inhabitants of the country do faint because of us.

Joshua 10:12-13
Then spake Joshua to the **Lord in the day when the Lord delivered up the Amorites before the children of Israel,** and he said in the sight of Israel, Sun, stand thou still upon Gibeon; and thou, Moon, in the valley of Ajalon. And the sun stood still, and the moon stayed, until the people had avenged themselves upon their enemies. Is not this written in the book of Jasher? So the sun stood still in the midst of heaven, and hasted not to go down about a whole day.

Joshua 10:19
And stay ye not, but pursue after your enemies, and smite the hindmost of them; **suffer them not to enter into their cities: for the Lord your God hath delivered them into your hand.**

Joshua 10:24
And it came to pass, when they brought out those kings unto Joshua, that Joshua called for all the men of Israel, and said unto the captains of the men of war which went with him, **Come near, put your feet upon the necks of these kings. And they came near, and put their feet upon the necks of them.**

Joshua 10:40
So Joshua smote all the country of the hills, and of the south, and of the vale, and of the springs, and all their kings: he left none remaining, **but utterly destroyed all that breathed, as the Lord God of Israel commanded.**

Joshua 10:42
And all these kings and their land did Joshua take at one time, because the Lord God of Israel fought for Israel.

Joshua 11:12
And all the cities of those kings, and all the kings of them, **did Joshua take, and smote them with the edge of the sword, and he utterly destroyed them,** as Moses the servant of the Lord commanded.

Joshua 11:18
Joshua made war a long time with all those kings.

Joshua 11:21
And at that time came Joshua, **and cut off the Anakims (Giants) from the mountains, from Hebron**, from Debir, from Anab, and from all the mountains of Judah, and from all the

mountains of Israel: Joshua destroyed them utterly with their cities.

Joshua 14:12
Now therefore give me this mountain, whereof the Lord spake in that day; for thou heardest in that day how the Anakims were there, and that the cities were great and fenced: **if so be the Lord will be with me, then I shall be able to drive them out, as the Lord said.**

Joshua 15:14
And **Caleb drove thence the three sons of Anak, Sheshai, and Ahiman, and Talmai, the children of Anak. (all giants)**

Joshua 23:10
One man of you shall chase a thousand: for the Lord your God, he it is that fighteth for you, as he hath promised you.

Joshua 13:12
All the kingdom of Og in Bashan, which reigned in Ashtaroth and in Edrei, **who remained of the remnant of the giants: for these did Moses smite, and cast them out.**

Joshua 21:44
And the Lord gave them rest round about,
according to all that he sware unto their fathers:
and there stood not a man of all their enemies
before them; **the Lord delivered all their
enemies into their hand.**

Joshua 24:5-7
I sent Moses also and Aaron, and I plagued
Egypt, according to that which I did among
them: and afterward **I brought you out.** And I
brought your fathers out of Egypt: and ye came
unto the sea; and the Egyptians pursued after
your fathers with chariots and horsemen unto the
Red sea. **And when they cried unto the Lord,
he put darkness between you and the
Egyptians, and brought the sea upon them,
and covered them;** and your eyes have seen
what I have done in Egypt: and ye dwelt in the
wilderness a long season.

The Book of Judges

Judges 1:2
And the Lord said, **Judah shall go up: behold,
I have delivered the land into his hand.**

Judges 1:4
And Judah went up; and the **Lord delivered the Canaanites and the Perizzites into their hand: and they slew of them in Bezek ten thousand men.**

Judges 2:16
Nevertheless the **Lord raised up judges, which delivered them out of the hand of those that spoiled them.**

Judges 2:18
And when the Lord raised them up judges, then the Lord was with the judge, **and delivered them out of the hand of their enemies all the days of the judge:** for it repented the Lord because of their groanings by reason of them that oppressed them and vexed them.

Judges 3:10
And the Spirit of the Lord came upon him, and he judged Israel, and went out to war: **and the Lord delivered Chushanrishathaim king of Mesopotamia into his hand; and his hand prevailed against Chushanrishathaim.**

Judges 3:15
But when the children of Israel cried unto the Lord, the **Lord raised them up a deliverer,**

Ehud the son of Gera, a Benjamite, a man lefthanded: and by him the children of Israel sent a present unto Eglon the king of Moab.

Judges 3:31
And after him was Shamgar the son of Anath, which slew of the Philistines six hundred men with an ox goad: **and he also delivered Israel.**

Judges 4:14
And Deborah said unto Barak, Up; for this is the day in which the **Lord hath delivered Sisera into thine hand:** is not the Lord gone out before thee? So Barak went down from mount Tabor, and ten thousand men after him.

Judges 7:7
And the Lord said unto Gideon, **By the three hundred men that lapped will I save you, and deliver the Midianites into thine hand:** and let all the other people go every man unto his place.

Judges 11:32
So Jephthah passed over unto the children of Ammon to fight against them; **and the Lord delivered them into his hands.**

The Books of 1 & 2 Samuel

1 Samuel 15:23
For **rebellion is as the sin of witchcraft, and stubbornness is as iniquity and idolatry.** Because thou hast rejected the word of the Lord, he hath also rejected thee from being king.

1 Samuel 17:45-51
Then said David to the Philistine, Thou comest to me with a sword, and with a spear, and with a shield: but **I come to thee in the name of the Lord of hosts, the God of the armies of Israel, whom thou hast defied. This day will the Lord deliver thee into mine hand; and I will smite thee, and take thine head from thee; and I will give the carcasses of the host of the Philistines this day unto the fowls of the air, and to the wild beasts of the earth; that all the earth may know that there is a God in Israel.** And all this assembly shall know that the Lord saveth not with sword and spear: for the battle is the Lord's, and he will give you into our hands. And it came to pass, when the Philistine arose, and came, and drew nigh to meet David, that David hastened, and ran toward the army to meet the Philistine. And David put his hand in his bag, and took thence a stone, and slang it, and smote the Philistine in his forehead, that the

stone sunk into his forehead; and he fell upon his face to the earth. **So David prevailed over the Philistine with a sling and with a stone, and smote the Philistine, and slew him; but there was no sword in the hand of David. Therefore David ran, and stood upon the Philistine, and took his sword, and drew it out of the sheath thereof, and slew him, and cut off his head therewith. And when the Philistines saw their champion was dead, they fled.**

1 Samuel 30:8
And David enquired at the Lord, saying, Shall I **pursue** after this troop? shall I overtake them? And he answered him, **Pursue: for thou shalt surely overtake them, and without fail recover all.**

2 Samuel 21:18
And it came to pass after this, that there was again a battle with the Philistines at Gob: **then Sibbechai the Hushathite slew Saph, which was of the sons of the giant.**

2 Samuel 21:19-22
And there was again a battle in Gob with the Philistines, where Elhanan the son of Jaareoregim, a Bethlehemite, slew the brother of

Goliath the Gittite, the staff of whose spear was like a weaver's beam. And there was yet a battle in Gath, where was a man of great stature, that had on every hand six fingers, and on every foot six toes, four and twenty in number; and he also was born to the giant. And when he defied Israel, **Jonathan the son of Shimeah the brother of David slew him. These four were born to the giant in Gath, and fell by the hand of David, and by the hand of his servants.**

2 Samuel 22:2
And he said, The Lord is my rock, and my fortress, **and my deliverer;**

2 Samuel 22:18
He delivered me from my strong enemy, and from them that hated me: for they were too strong for me.

2 Samuel 22:20
He brought me forth also into a large place: **he delivered me**, because he delighted in me.

2 Samuel 22:49
And that bringeth me forth from mine enemies: thou also hast lifted me up on high above them that rose up against me: **thou hast delivered me from the violent man.**

The Books of 1 & 2 Kings

<u>1 Kings 14:24</u>
And there were also **sodomites** in the land: and they did according to all the abominations of the nations which the Lord **cast out before the children of Israel.**

<u>1 Kings 21:26</u>
And he did very abominably in following idols, according to all things as did the Amorites, **whom the Lord cast out before the children of Israel.**

<u>2 Kings 9:22</u>
And it came to pass, when Joram saw Jehu, that he said, Is it peace, Jehu? And he answered, **What peace, so long as the whoredoms of thy mother Jezebel and her witchcrafts are so many?**

The Books of 1 & 2 Chronicles

<u>1 Chronicles 14:11</u>
So they came up to Baalperazim; and David smote them there. Then David said, **God hath broken in upon mine enemies by mine hand**

like the breaking forth of waters: therefore they called the name of that place Baalperazim.

2 Chronicles 11:15
And he ordained him priests for the high places, and for the devils, and for the calves which he had made.

2 Chronicles 33:6
And he caused his children to pass through the fire in the valley of the son of Hinnom: also he observed times, and used enchantments, and used witchcraft, and dealt with a familiar spirit, and with wizards: **he wrought much evil in the sight of the Lord, to provoke him to anger.**

The Book of Esther

Esther 4:14
For if thou altogether holdest thy peace at this time, **then shall there enlargement and deliverance arise to the Jews from another place;** but thou and thy father's house shall be destroyed: and who knoweth whether thou art come to the kingdom for such a time as this?

The Book of Job

<u>Job 29:17</u>
And **I brake the jaws of the wicked, and plucked the spoil out of his teeth.**

<u>Job 42:10</u>
And the **Lord turned the captivity of Job,** when he prayed for his friends: also the Lord gave Job twice as much as he had before.

The Book of Psalm

<u>Psalm 3:7</u>
Arise, O Lord; save me, O my God: **for thou hast smitten all mine enemies upon the cheek bone; thou hast broken the teeth of the ungodly.**

<u>Psalm 5:10</u>
Destroy thou them, O God; let them fall by their own counsels; cast them out in the multitude of their transgressions; for they have rebelled against thee.

<u>Psalm 6:4</u>
Return, O Lord, **deliver my soul:** oh save me for thy mercies' sake.

Psalm 7:1
O Lord my God, in thee do I put my trust: save me from all them that persecute me, **and deliver me:**

Psalm 7:2
Lest he tear my soul like a lion, rending it in pieces, **while there is none to deliver.**

Psalm 9:9
The Lord also will be a refuge for the oppressed, a **refuge** in times of trouble.

Psalm 14:7
Oh that the salvation of Israel were come out of Zion! **when the Lord bringeth back the captivity of his people,** Jacob shall rejoice, and Israel shall be glad.

Psalm 17:13
Arise, O Lord, disappoint him, cast him down: **deliver my soul from the wicked**, which is thy sword:

Psalm 18:2
The Lord is my rock, and my fortress, **and my deliverer**; my God, my strength, in whom I will trust; my buckler, and the horn of my salvation, and my high tower.

Psalm 18:3
I will call upon the Lord, who is worthy to be praised: **so shall I be saved from mine enemies.**

Psalm 18:16
He sent from above, he took me, **he drew me out of many waters.**

Psalm 18:17
He delivered me from my strong enemy, and from them which hated me: for they were too strong for me.

Psalm 18:19
He brought me forth also into a large place**; he delivered me, because he delighted in me.**

Psalm 18:27
For **thou wilt save the afflicted people**; but wilt bring down high looks.

Psalm 18:34
He teacheth my hands to war, so that a bow of steel is broken by mine arms.

Psalm 18:40
Thou hast also given me the necks of mine enemies; that I might destroy them that hate me.

Psalm 18:42
Then did I beat them small as the dust before the wind: **I did cast them out as the dirt in the streets.**

Psalm 18:50
Great deliverance giveth he to his king; and sheweth mercy to his anointed, to David, and to his seed for evermore.

Psalm 22:20
Deliver my soul from the sword; my darling from the power of the dog.

Psalm 22:21
Save me from the lion's mouth: for thou hast heard me from the horns of the unicorns.

Psalm 22:24
For he hath not despised nor abhorred the affliction of the afflicted; neither hath he hid his face from him; but when he cried unto him, he heard.

Psalm 23:3
He restoreth my soul...

Psalm 25:2
O my God, I trust in thee: let me not be ashamed, **let not mine enemies triumph over me.**

Psalm 25:20
O keep my soul, and deliver me: let me not be ashamed; for I put my trust in thee.

Psalm 27:1
The Lord is my light and my salvation; whom shall I fear? **the Lord is the strength of my life; of whom shall I be afraid?**

Psalm 27:2
When the wicked, even mine enemies and my foes, came upon me to eat up my flesh, **they stumbled and fell.**

Psalm 31:1
In thee, O Lord, do I put my trust; let me never be ashamed: **deliver me in thy righteousness.**

Psalm 31:2
Bow down thine ear to me; **deliver me speedily:** be thou my strong rock, for an house of defence to save me.

Psalm 31:15
My times are in thy hand: **deliver me from the hand of mine enemies, and from them that persecute me.**

Psalm 32:7
Thou art my hiding place; thou shalt preserve me from trouble; **thou shalt compass me about with songs of deliverance. Selah.**

Psalm 33:19
To deliver their soul from death, and to keep them alive in famine.

Psalm 34:4
I sought the Lord, and he heard me, **and delivered me from all my fears.**

Psalm 34:7
The angel of the Lord encampeth round about them that fear him, **and delivereth them.**

Psalm 34:17
The righteous cry, and the Lord heareth, **and delivereth them out of all their troubles.**

Psalm 34:18
The Lord is nigh unto them that are of a broken heart; and saveth such as be of a contrite spirit.

Psalm 34:19
Many are the afflictions of the righteous: **but the Lord delivereth him out of them all.**

Psalm 35:1
Plead my cause, O Lord, with them that strive with me: fight against them that fight against me.

Psalm 35:10
All my bones shall say, Lord, **who is like unto thee, which deliverest the poor from him that is too strong for him,** yea, the poor and the needy from him that spoileth him?

Psalm 37:20
But the wicked shall perish, and the enemies of the Lord shall be as the fat of lambs: **they shall consume; into smoke shall they consume away.**

Psalm 37:40
And the Lord shall help them, **and deliver them: he shall deliver them from the wicked**, and save them, because they trust in him.

Psalm 38:22
Make haste to help me, O Lord my salvation.

Psalm 40:2
He brought me up also out of an horrible pit, out of the miry clay, and set my feet upon a rock, and established my goings.

Psalm 40:13
Be pleased, O Lord, **to deliver me:** O Lord, make haste to help me.

Psalm 40:17
But I am poor and needy; yet the Lord thinketh upon me: **thou art my help and my deliverer;** make no tarrying, O my God.

Psalm 41:1
Blessed is he that considereth the poor: **the Lord will deliver him in time of trouble.**

Psalm 41:2
The Lord will preserve him, and keep him alive; and he shall be blessed upon the earth: and

thou wilt not deliver him unto the will of his enemies.

Psalm 44:4
Thou art my King, O God: **command deliverances for Jacob.**

Psalm 44:5
Through thee will we push down our enemies: through thy name will we tread them under that rise up against us.

Psalm 44:7
But thou hast saved us from our enemies, and hast put them to shame that hated us.

Psalm 50:15
And call upon me in the day of trouble: **I will deliver thee, and thou shalt glorify me.**

Psalm 50:22
Now consider this, ye that forget God, lest I tear you in pieces, and there be none to deliver.

Psalm 51:12
Restore unto me the joy of thy salvation; and uphold me with thy free spirit.

Psalm 51:17
The sacrifices of God are a broken spirit: a broken and a contrite heart, O God, thou wilt not despise.

Psalm 58:6
Break their teeth, O God, in their mouth: **break out the great teeth of the young lions,** O Lord.

Psalm 66:3
Say unto God, How terrible art thou in thy works! **through the greatness of thy power shall thine enemies submit themselves unto thee.**

Psalm 68:1
Let God arise, let his enemies be scattered: let them also that hate him flee before him.

Psalm 68:6
God setteth the solitary in families: he bringeth out those which are bound with chains: but the rebellious dwell in a dry land.

Psalm 69:1
Save me, O God; for the waters are come in unto my soul.

Psalm 69:14
Deliver me out of the mire, and let me not sink: **let me be delivered from them that hate me**, and out of the deep waters.

Psalm 69:15
Let not the waterflood overflow me, neither let the deep swallow me up, and **let not** the pit shut her mouth upon me.

Psalm 69:18
Draw nigh unto my soul, and redeem it: **deliver me because of mine enemies.**

Psalm 69:33
For the Lord heareth the poor, **and despiseth not his prisoners.**

Psalm 70:1
Make haste, O God, to deliver me; make haste to help me, O Lord.

Psalm 70:5
But I am poor and needy: make haste unto me, O God: **thou art my help and my deliverer;** O Lord, make no tarrying.

Psalm 71:2
Deliver me in thy righteousness, and cause me to escape: incline thine ear unto me, and save me.

Psalm 71:4
Deliver me, O my God, out of the hand of the wicked, out of the hand of the unrighteous and cruel man.

Psalm 71:12
O God, be not far from me: **O my God, make haste for my help.**

Psalm 72:9
They that dwell in the wilderness shall bow before him; **and his enemies shall lick the dust**.

Psalm 72:12
For he shall deliver the needy when he crieth; the poor also, and him that hath no helper.

Psalm 74:12
For God is my King of old, working salvation in the midst of the earth.

Psalm 74:13
Thou didst divide the sea by thy strength: **thou brakest the heads of the dragons in the waters.**

Psalm 79:11
Let the sighing of the prisoner come before thee; according to the greatness of thy power preserve thou those that are appointed to die;

Psalm 81:7
Thou calledst in trouble, and I delivered thee; I answered thee in the secret place of thunder: I proved thee at the waters of Meribah. Selah.

Psalm 82:4
Deliver the poor and needy: rid them out of the hand of the wicked.

Psalm 85:1
Lord, thou hast been favourable unto thy land: **thou hast brought back the captivity of Jacob.**

Psalm 86:13
For great is thy mercy toward me: **and thou hast delivered my soul from the lowest hell.**

Psalm 86:17
Shew me a token for good; that they which hate me may see it, and be ashamed: **because thou, Lord, hast helped me, and comforted me.**

Psalm 89:10
Thou hast broken Rahab in pieces, as one that is slain; **thou hast scattered** thine enemies with thy strong arm.

Psalm 89:23
And **I will beat down his foes before his face**, and plague them that hate him.

Psalm 91:3
Surely he shall deliver thee from the snare of the fowler, and from the noisome pestilence.

Psalm 91:13
Thou shalt tread upon the lion and adder: the young lion and the dragon shalt thou trample under feet.

Psalm 91:14
Because he hath set his love upon me, therefore will I deliver him: I will set him on high, because he hath known my name.

Psalm 91:15
He shall call upon me, and I will answer him: I will be with him in trouble; **I will deliver him, and honour him.**

Psalm 97:3
A fire (glory-fire) goeth before him, and burneth up his enemies round about.

Psalm 97:10
Ye that love the Lord, hate evil: **he preserveth the souls of his saints; he delivereth them out of the hand of the wicked.**

Psalm 102:20
To hear the groaning of the prisoner; **to loose those that are appointed to death;**

Psalm 105:20
The king sent and **loosed him**; even the ruler of the people, **and let him go free.**

Psalm 106:9
He rebuked the **Red sea** also, and it was dried up: so he led them through the depths, as through the wilderness.

Psalm 106:10
And he saved them from the hand of him that hated them, **and redeemed them** from the hand of the enemy.

Psalm 106:11
And the waters covered their enemies: there was not one of them left.

Psalm 106:37
Yea, they sacrificed their sons and their daughters **unto devils,**

Psalm 107:6
Then they cried unto the Lord in their trouble, **and he delivered them out of their distresses.**

Psalm 107:9-11
For he satisfieth the longing soul, and filleth the hungry soul with goodness. Such as sit in darkness and in the shadow of death, being bound in affliction and iron; Because they rebelled against the words of God, and contemned the counsel of the most High:

Psalm 107:17
Fools because of their transgression, and because of their iniquities, **are afflicted.**

Psalm 107:20
He sent his word, and healed them, **and delivered them from their destructions.**

Psalm 108:6
That thy beloved may be delivered: save with thy right hand, and answer me.

Psalm 109:26
Help me, O Lord my God: O save me according to thy mercy:

Psalm 110:2
The Lord shall send the rod of thy strength out of Zion: **rule thou in the midst of thine enemies.**

Psalm 136:13-15
To him which divided the Red sea into parts: for his mercy endureth for ever: And made Israel to pass through the midst of it: for his mercy endureth for ever: **But overthrew Pharaoh and his host in the Red sea: for his mercy endureth for ever.**

Psalm 116:4
Then called I upon the name of the Lord; **O Lord, I beseech thee, deliver my soul.**

Psalm 116:8
For thou hast delivered my soul from death, mine eyes from tears, and my feet from falling.

Psalm 116:16
O Lord, truly I am thy servant; I am thy servant, and the son of thine handmaid: **thou hast loosed my bonds.**

Psalm 118:7
The Lord taketh my part with them that help me: therefore shall I see my desire upon them that hate me.

Psalm 118:17
I shall not die, but live, and declare the works of the Lord.

Psalm 119:134
Deliver me from the oppression of man: so will I keep thy precepts.

Psalm 119:153
Consider mine affliction, and deliver me: for I do not forget thy law.

Psalm 119:154
Plead my cause, and deliver me: quicken me according to thy word.

Psalm 119:170
Let my supplication come before thee: **deliver me according to thy word.**

Psalm 120:2
Deliver my soul, O Lord, from lying lips, and from a deceitful tongue.

Psalm 124:6
Blessed be the Lord, who hath not given us as a prey to their teeth.

Psalm 124:7
Our soul is escaped as a bird out of the snare of the fowlers: the snare is broken, **and we are escaped.**

Psalm 126:1
When the Lord turned again the captivity of Zion, we were like them that dream.

Psalm 126:4
Turn again our captivity, O Lord, as the streams in the south.

Psalm 129:5
Let them all be confounded and turned back that hate Zion.

Psalm 138:7

Though I walk in the midst of trouble, **thou wilt revive me**: thou shalt stretch forth thine hand against the wrath of mine enemies, and thy right hand shall save me.

Psalm 140:1

Deliver me, O Lord, from the evil man: preserve me from the violent man;

Psalm 142:6

Attend unto my cry; for I am brought very low: **deliver me from my persecutors**; for they are stronger than I.

Psalm 142:7

Bring my soul out of prison, that I may praise thy name: the righteous shall compass me about; for thou shalt deal bountifully with me.

Psalm 143:7

Hear me speedily, O Lord: my spirit faileth: hide not thy face from me, lest I be like unto them that go down into the pit.

Psalm 143:9

Deliver me, O Lord, from mine enemies: I flee unto thee to hide me.

Psalm 143:12
**And of thy mercy cut off mine enemies, and
destroy all them that afflict my soul: for I am
thy servant.**

Psalm 144:1
Blessed be the Lord my strength **which
teacheth my hands to war, and my fingers to
fight:**

Psalm 144:2
My goodness, and my fortress; my high tower,
and my deliverer; my shield, and he in whom I
trust; who subdueth my people under me.

Psalm 144:7
Send thine hand from above; rid me, **and deliver
me out of great waters,** from the hand of
strange children;

Psalm 144:10
It is he that giveth salvation unto kings: **who
delivereth David his servant from the hurtful
sword.**

Psalm 144:11
**Rid me, and deliver me from the hand of
strange children,** whose mouth speaketh vanity,
and their right hand is a right hand of falsehood:

Psalm 146:7
Which executeth judgment for the oppressed: which giveth food to the hungry. **The Lord looseth the prisoners:**

Psalm 149:8
To bind their kings with chains, and their nobles with fetters of iron;

The Book of Proverbs

Proverbs 2:12
To deliver thee from the way of the evil man, from the man that speaketh froward things;

Proverbs 2:16
To deliver thee from the strange woman, even from the stranger which flattereth with her words;

Proverbs 18:14
The spirit of a man will sustain his infirmity; but a wounded spirit who can bear?

Proverbs 26:2
As the bird by wandering, as the swallow by flying, **so the curse causeless shall not come.**

The Book of Ecclesiastes

Ecclesiastes 10:8
He that diggeth a pit shall fall into it; and whoso breaketh an hedge, a serpent shall bite him.

The Book of Isaiah

Isaiah 4:6
And there shall be a tabernacle for a shadow in the day time from the heat, **and for a place of refuge, and for a covert from storm and from rain.**

Isaiah 10:27
And it shall come to pass in that day, that his burden shall be taken away from off thy shoulder, **and his yoke from off thy neck, and the yoke shall be destroyed because of the anointing.**

Isaiah 25:4
For thou hast been a strength to the poor, a strength to the needy in his distress, **a refuge from the storm, a shadow from the heat,** when the blast of the terrible ones is as a storm against the wall.

Isaiah 27:1
In that day the Lord with his sore and great and strong sword shall punish leviathan the

piercing serpent, even leviathan that crooked serpent; and he shall slay the dragon that is in the sea.

Isaiah 28:18
And your covenant with death shall be disannulled, and your agreement with hell shall not stand; when the overflowing scourge shall pass through, then ye shall be trodden down by it.

Isaiah 42:7
To open the blind eyes, to bring out the prisoners from the prison, and them that sit in darkness out of the prison house.

Isaiah 42:13
The Lord shall go forth as a mighty man, he shall stir up jealousy like a man of war: he shall cry, yea, roar; he shall prevail against his enemies.

Isaiah 42:22
But this is a people robbed and spoiled; they are all of them snared in holes, and they are hid in prison houses: they are for a prey, **and none delivereth; for a spoil, and none saith, Restore.**

Isaiah 44:25
That frustrateth the tokens of the liars, and maketh diviners mad; that turneth wise men backward, and maketh their knowledge foolish;

Isaiah 45:13
I have raised him up in righteousness, and I will direct all his ways: he shall build my city, **and he shall let go my captives, not for price nor reward, saith the Lord of hosts**.

Isaiah 46:4
And even to your old age I am he; and even to hoar hairs will I carry you: I have made, **and I will bear; even I will carry, and will deliver you**.

Isaiah 48:20
Go ye forth of Babylon, flee ye from the Chaldeans, with a voice of singing declare ye, tell this, utter it even to the end of the earth; say ye, The Lord hath redeemed his servant Jacob.

Isaiah 49:9
That thou mayest say to the prisoners, Go forth; to them that are in darkness, Shew yourselves. They shall feed in the ways, and their pastures shall be in all high places.

Isaiah 49:13

Sing, O heavens; and be joyful, O earth; and break forth into singing, O mountains: **for the Lord hath comforted his people, and will have mercy upon his afflicted.**

Isaiah 49:25

But thus saith the Lord, **Even the captives of the mighty shall be taken away, and the prey of the terrible shall be delivered:** for I will contend with him that contendeth with thee, and I will save thy children.

Isaiah 51:9

Awake, awake, put on strength, O arm of the Lord; awake, as in the ancient days, in the generations of old. **Art thou not it that hath cut Rahab, and wounded the dragon?**

Isaiah 52:2

Shake thyself from the dust; arise, and sit down, O Jerusalem: **loose thyself** from the bands of thy neck, **O captive daughter of Zion.**

Isaiah 53:5

But he was wounded for our transgressions, he was bruised for our iniquities: the chastisement of our peace was upon him; and with his stripes we are healed.

Isaiah 54:11
O thou afflicted, tossed with tempest, and not comforted, behold, I will lay thy stones with fair colors, and lay thy foundations with sapphires.

Isaiah 57:15
For thus saith the high and lofty One that inhabiteth eternity, whose name is Holy; I dwell in the high and holy place, with him also that is of a contrite and humble spirit, **to revive the spirit of the humble, and to revive the heart of the contrite ones.**

Isaiah 58:6
Is not this the fast that I have chosen? to loose the bands of wickedness, to undo the heavy burdens, and to let the oppressed go free, and that ye break every yoke?

Isaiah 59:19
So shall they fear the name of the Lord from the west, and his glory from the rising of the sun. **When the enemy shall come in like a flood, the Spirit of the Lord shall lift up a standard against him.**

Isaiah 61:1
The Spirit of the Lord God is upon me; because the Lord hath anointed me to preach

good tidings unto the meek; he hath sent me to bind up the brokenhearted, to proclaim liberty to the captives, and the opening of the prison to them that are bound;

Isaiah 63:9
In all their affliction he was afflicted, and the angel of his presence saved them: **in his love and in his pity he redeemed them; and he bare them, and carried them all the days of old.**

Isaiah 66:2
For all those things hath mine hand made, and all those things have been, saith the Lord: **but to this man will I look, even to him that is poor and of a contrite spirit, and trembleth at my word.**

The Book of Jeremiah

Jeremiah 6:14
They have healed also the hurt of the daughter of my people slightly, saying, Peace, peace; when there is no peace.

Jeremiah 8:11

For they have healed the hurt of the daughter of my people slightly, saying, Peace, peace; when there is no peace.

Jeremiah 29:10

For thus saith the Lord, That after seventy years be accomplished at Babylon **I will visit you, and perform my good word toward you, in causing you to return to this place.**

Jeremiah 34:9

That every man should let his manservant, and every man his maidservant, being an Hebrew or an Hebrewess, **go free**; that none should serve himself of them, to wit, of a Jew his brother.

Jeremiah 51:20

Thou art my battle axe and weapons of war: for with thee will I break in pieces the nations, and with thee will I destroy kingdoms;

The Book of Daniel

Daniel 3:17

If it be so, our God whom we serve is able to deliver us from the burning fiery furnace, and he will deliver us out of thine hand, O king.

Daniel 3:26
Then Nebuchadnezzar came near to the mouth of the burning fiery furnace, and spake, and said, Shadrach, Meshach, and Abednego, ye servants of the most high God, come forth, and come hither. **Then Shadrach, Meshach, and Abednego, came forth of the midst of the fire.**

Daniel 6:22
My God hath sent his angel, and hath shut the lions' mouths, that they have not hurt me: forasmuch as before him innocency was found in me; and also before thee, O king, have I done no hurt.

Daniel 10:12-13
Then said he unto me, Fear not, Daniel: for from the first day that thou didst set thine heart to understand, and to chasten thyself before thy God, thy words were heard, and I am come for thy words.
But the Prince of the kingdom of Persia withstood me one and twenty days: but, lo, Michael, one of the chief princes, came to help me; and I remained there with the king of Persia.

The Book of Joel

Joel 2:32
And it shall come to pass, **that whosoever shall call on the name of the Lord shall be delivered: for in mount Zion and in Jerusalem shall be deliverance,** as the Lord hath said, and in the remnant whom the Lord shall call.

Joel 2:25
And I will restore to you the years that the locust hath eaten, the cankerworm, and the caterpillar, and the palmerworm, my great army which I sent among you.

The Book of Obadiah

Obadiah 1:17
But upon mount Zion shall be deliverance, and there shall be holiness; and the house of Jacob shall possess their possessions.

Obadiah 1:21
And saviors (deliverers) shall come upon Mount Zion to judge the mount of Esau; and the Kingdom shall be the Lord's.

The Book of Micah

<u>Micah 5:12</u>
And I will cut off witchcrafts out of thine hand; and **thou shalt have no more** soothsayers:

The Book of Nahum

<u>Nahum 3:4</u>
Because of the multitude of the whoredoms of the wellfavoured harlot, the mistress of witchcrafts, that selleth nations through her whoredoms, and families through her witchcrafts.

The Book of Zechariah

<u>Zechariah 3:2</u>
And the Lord said unto Satan, **The Lord rebuke thee, O Satan**; even the Lord that hath chosen Jerusalem rebuke thee: is not this a brand plucked out of the fire?

<u>Zechariah 10:2</u>
For the idols have spoken vanity, and the diviners have seen a lie, and have told false dreams; they comfort in vain: therefore they went

their way as a flock, they were troubled, because there was no shepherd.

Zechariah 10:3
Mine anger was kindled against the shepherds, and I punished the goats: **for the Lord of hosts hath visited his flock the house of Judah, and hath made them as his goodly horse in the battle.**

The Book of Malachi

Malachi 4:2
But unto you that fear my name shall the Sun of righteousness arise with healing in his wings; **and ye shall go forth, and grow up as calves of the stall.**

The Book of Matthew

Matthew 7:5
Thou hypocrite, **first cast out the beam out of thine own eye;** and then shalt thou see clearly to cast out the mote out of thy brother's eye.

Matthew 4:24
And his fame went throughout all Syria: and **they brought unto him all sick people that were taken with divers diseases and torments, and those which were possessed with devils, and those which were lunatick, and those that had the palsy; and he healed them.**

Matthew 6:13
And lead us not into temptation, **but deliver us from evil:** For thine is the kingdom, and the power, and the glory, for ever. Amen.

Matthew 7:21-23
Not every one that saith unto me, Lord, Lord, shall enter into the kingdom of heaven; but he that doeth the will of my Father which is in heaven. **Many will say to me in that day, Lord, Lord, have we not prophesied in thy name? and in thy name have cast out devils?** and in thy name done many wonderful works?
And **then will I profess unto them, I never knew you: depart from me, ye that work iniquity.**

Matthew 8:16
When the even was come, **they brought unto him many that were possessed with devils:**

and he cast out the spirits with his word, and healed all that were sick:

Matthew 8:28
And when he was come to the other side into the country of the Gergesenes, **there met him two possessed with devils, coming out of the tombs, exceeding fierce, so that no man might pass by that way.**

Matthew 8:31
So the devils besought him, saying, If thou cast us out, suffer us to go away into the herd of swine.

Matthew 8:33
And they that kept them fled, and went their ways into the city, and told every thing, **and what was befallen to the possessed of the devils.**

Matthew 9:32
As they went out, behold, **they brought to him a dumb man possessed with a devil.**

Matthew 9:33
And when the devil was cast out, the dumb spake: and the multitudes marveled, saying, It was never so seen in Israel.

Matthew 10:1

And when he had called unto him his twelve disciples, **he gave them power against unclean spirits, to cast them out,** and to heal all manner of sickness and all manner of disease.

Matthew 10:8

Heal the sick, cleanse the lepers, raise the dead, cast out devils: freely ye have received, freely give.

Matthew 12:22

Then was brought unto him one possessed with a devil, blind, and dumb: and he healed him, insomuch that the blind and dumb both spake and saw.

Matthew 12:23-26

And all the people were amazed, and said, Is not this the son of David?
But when the Pharisees heard it, they said, This fellow doth not cast out devils, but by Beelzebub the prince of the devils.

And Jesus knew their thoughts, and said unto them, **Every kingdom divided against itself is brought to desolation; and every city or house divided against itself shall not stand:**

And **if Satan cast out Satan, he is divided against himself; how shall then his kingdom stand?**

Matthew 12:28
But **if I cast out devils by the Spirit of God, then the kingdom of God is come unto you.**

Matthew 12:43
When the unclean spirit is gone out of a man, he walketh through dry places, seeking rest, and findeth none.

Matthew 15:22
And, behold, a woman of Canaan came out of the same coasts, and cried unto him, saying, Have mercy on me, **O Lord, thou son of David; my daughter is grievously vexed with a devil.**

Matthew 15:26-28
But he answered and said, **It is not meet to take the children's bread, and to cast it to dogs.** And she said, Truth, Lord: **yet the dogs eat of the crumbs which fall from their masters' table.** Then Jesus answered and said unto her, **O woman, great is thy faith: be it unto thee even as thou wilt. And her daughter was made whole from that very hour.**

Matthew 17:15

Lord, have mercy on my son: **for he is lunatick, and sore vexed:** for ofttimes he falleth into the fire, and oft into the water.

Matthew 17:18

And Jesus rebuked the devil; and he departed out of him: and the child was cured from that very hour.

The Book of Mark

Mark 1:23

And there was in their synagogue a man with an unclean spirit; and he cried out,

Mark 1:26

And when the unclean spirit had torn him, and cried with a loud voice, he came out of him.

Mark 1:27

And they were all amazed, insomuch that they questioned among themselves, saying, What thing is this? what new doctrine is this? **for with authority commandeth he even the unclean spirits, and they do obey him.**

Mark 1:32
And at even, when the sun did set, **they brought unto him all that were diseased, and them that were possessed with devils.**

Mark 1:34
And he healed many that were **sick of divers diseases, and cast out many devils; and suffered not the devils to speak, because they knew him.**

Mark 1:39
And he preached in their synagogues throughout all Galilee, **and cast out devils.**

Mark 3:11
And unclean spirits, when they saw him, fell down before him, and cried, saying, Thou art the Son of God.

Mark 3:15
And to have power to heal sicknesses, **and to cast out devils:**

Mark 5:2
And when he was come out of the ship, **immediately there met him out of the tombs a man with an unclean spirit,**

Mark 5:9
And he asked him, **What is thy name? And he answered, saying, My name is Legion: for we are many.**

Mark 5:13
And **forthwith Jesus gave them leave. And the unclean spirits went out, and entered into the swine: and the herd ran violently down a steep place into the sea, (they were about two thousand;) and were choked in the sea.**

Mark 5:15
And they come to Jesus, **and see him that was possessed with the devil, and had the legion, sitting, and clothed, and in his right mind:** and they were afraid.

Mark 5:18-19
And when he was come into the ship, **he that had been possessed with the devil prayed him that he might be with him.** Howbeit Jesus suffered him not, but saith unto him, Go home to thy friends, and tell them how great things the Lord hath done for thee, and hath had compassion on thee.

Mark 6:13

And they cast out many devils, and anointed with oil many that were sick, and healed them.

Mark 7:26

The woman was a Greek, a Syrophenician by nation; and **she besought him that he would cast forth the devil out of her daughter.**

Mark 7:29

And he said unto her, For this saying go thy way; **the devil is gone out of thy daughter.**

Mark 7:30

And when she was come to her house, **she found the devil gone out, and her daughter laid upon the bed.**

Mark 9:18

And wheresoever he taketh him, he teareth him: and he foameth, and gnasheth with his teeth, and pineth away: and **I spake to thy disciples that they should cast him out; and they could not.**

Mark 9:25

When Jesus saw that the people came running together, **he rebuked the foul spirit, saying unto him, Thou dumb and deaf spirit, I**

charge thee, come out of him, and enter no more into him.

Mark 9:28-29
And when he was come into the house, his disciples asked him privately, Why could not we cast him out? **And he said unto them, This kind can come forth by nothing, but by prayer and fasting.**

Mark 9:38-39
And John answered him, saying, **Master, we saw one casting out devils in thy name, and he followeth not us: and we forbad him, because he followeth not us. But Jesus said, Forbid him not: for there is no man which shall do a miracle in my name, that can lightly speak evil of me.**

Mark 16:9
Now when Jesus was risen early the first day of the week, **he appeared first to Mary Magdalene, out of whom he had cast seven devils.**

Mark 16:17
And these signs shall follow them that believe; In my name shall they cast out devils; they shall speak with new tongues;

The Book of Luke

Luke 1:70-72
As he spake by the mouth of his holy prophets, which have been since the world began: **That we should be saved from our enemies, and from the hand of all that hate us;** To perform the mercy promised to our fathers, and to remember his holy covenant;

Luke 4:18
The Spirit of the Lord is upon me, because he hath anointed me to preach the gospel to the poor; he hath sent me to heal the brokenhearted, to preach deliverance to the captives, and recovering of sight to the blind, to set at liberty them that are bruised,

Luke 4:33
And **in the synagogue there was a man, which had a spirit of an unclean devil, and cried out with a loud voice,**

Luke 4:35
And Jesus rebuked him, saying, **Hold thy peace, and come out of him. And when the devil had thrown him in the midst, he came out of him, and hurt him not.**

Luke 6:18
And **they that were vexed with unclean spirits**: and they were healed.

Luke 7:21
And in that same hour he cured many of their infirmities and plagues, **and of evil spirits; and unto many that were blind he gave sight.**

Luke 8:2
And certain women, which had been healed of evil spirits and infirmities, **Mary called Magdalene, out of whom went seven devils,**

Luke 10:18
And he said unto them, **I beheld Satan as lightning fall from heaven.**

Luke 10:19
Behold, I give unto you power to tread on serpents and scorpions, and over all the power of the enemy: and nothing shall by any means hurt you.

Luke 11:20
But if I with the finger of God cast out devils, no doubt the kingdom of God is come upon you.

Luke 13:12
And when Jesus saw her, he called her to him, and said unto her, **Woman, thou art loosed from thine infirmity.**

Luke 13:16
And ought not this woman, being a daughter of Abraham, **whom Satan hath bound,** lo, these **eighteen years, be loosed from this bond on the Sabbath day?**

Luke 13:32
And he said unto them, **Go ye, and tell that fox, Behold, I cast out devils, and I do cures to day and to morrow, and the third day I shall be perfected.**

The Book of John

John 8:36
If the Son therefore shall make you free, ye shall be free indeed.

John 8:44
Ye are of your father the devil, and the lusts of your father ye will do. He was a murderer from the beginning, and abode not in the truth, because there is no truth in him. When

he speaketh a lie, he speaketh of his own: for he is a liar, and the father of it.

John 11:44
And he that was dead came forth, bound hand and foot with grave clothes: and his face was bound about with a napkin. **Jesus saith unto them, Loose him, and let him go.**

The Book of Acts

Acts 5:16
There came also a multitude out of the cities round about unto Jerusalem, bringing sick folks, and **them which were vexed with unclean spirits**: and they were healed every one.

Acts 5:19
But the **angel of the Lord by night opened the prison doors, and brought them forth,** and said,

Acts 7:36
He brought them out, after that he had shewed wonders and signs in the land of Egypt, and in the Red sea, and in the wilderness forty years.

Acts 8:7

For unclean spirits, crying with loud voice, came out of many that were possessed with them: and many taken with palsies, and that were lame, were healed.

Acts 10:38

How God anointed Jesus of Nazareth with the Holy Ghost and with power: who went about doing good, and healing all that were oppressed of the devil; for God was with him.

Acts 13:10

And said, **O full of all subtilty and all mischief, thou child of the devil, thou enemy of all righteousness, wilt thou not cease to pervert the right ways of the Lord?**

Acts 16:16-18

And it came to pass, as we went to prayer, **a certain damsel possessed with a spirit of divination met us, which brought her masters much gain by soothsaying:** The same followed Paul and us, and cried, saying, These men are the servants of the most high God, which shew unto us the way of salvation. And this did she many days. But Paul, **being grieved, turned and said to the spirit, I command thee** in the name of Jesus Christ to come out of her. And he came out the same hour.

Acts 16:25-26
And at midnight Paul and Silas prayed, and sang praises unto God: and the prisoners heard them. **And suddenly there was a great earthquake, so that the foundations of the prison were shaken: and immediately all the doors were opened, and every one's bands were loosed.**

Acts 19:12
So that from his body were brought unto the sick handkerchiefs or aprons, and the diseases departed from them, **and the evil spirits went out of them.**

Acts 19:13-16
Then certain of the vagabond Jews, exorcists, took upon them to call over them which had evil spirits the name of the Lord Jesus, saying, We adjure you by Jesus whom Paul preacheth. And there were seven sons of one Sceva, a Jew, and chief of the priests, which did so. And the evil spirit answered and said, Jesus I know, and Paul I know; but who are ye? And the man in whom the evil spirit was leaped on them, and overcame them, and

prevailed against them, so that they fled out of that house naked and wounded.

The Book of Romans

Romans 8:15
For ye have not received the spirit of bondage again to fear; but ye have received the Spirit of adoption, whereby we cry, Abba, Father.

Romans 16:20
And the God of peace shall bruise Satan under your feet shortly. The grace of our Lord Jesus Christ be with you. Amen.

The Books of 1 & 2 Corinthians

1 Corinthians 5:7
Purge out therefore the old leaven, that ye may be a new lump, as ye are unleavened. For even Christ our passover is sacrificed for us:

1 Corinthians 10:20
But I say, that the things which the Gentiles sacrifice, they sacrifice to devils, and not to God: **and I would not that ye should have fellowship with devils.**

1 Corinthians 10:21
Ye cannot drink the cup of the Lord, and the cup of devils: ye cannot be partakers of the Lord's table, and of the table of devils.

2 Corinthians 1:10
Who delivered us from so great a death, and doth deliver: in whom we trust that he will yet deliver us;

2 Corinthians 2:11
Lest Satan should get an advantage of us: for we are not ignorant of his devices.

2 Corinthians 3:17
Now the Lord is that Spirit: and where the Spirit of the Lord is, there is liberty.

2 Corinthians 10:4
(For the weapons of our warfare are not carnal, but mighty through God to the pulling down of strong holds;)

2 Corinthians 11:14
And no marvel; for Satan himself is transformed into an angel of light.

The Book of Galatians

Galatians 1:4
Who gave himself for our sins, **that he might deliver us from this present evil world**, according to the will of God and our Father:

Galatians 3:13
Christ hath redeemed us from the curse of the law, being made a curse for us: for it is written, Cursed is every one that hangeth on a tree:

Galatians 5:1
Stand fast therefore in the liberty wherewith Christ hath made us free, and be not entangled again with the yoke of bondage.

The Book of Ephesians

Ephesians 1:20-22
Which he wrought in Christ, when he raised him from the dead, and set him at his own right hand in the heavenly places, **Far above all principality, and power, and might, and dominion, and every name that is named, not only in this world, but also in that which is to come:** And hath put all things under his feet, and

gave him to be the head over all things to the church,

Ephesians 4:27
Neither give place to the devil.

Ephesians 6:11-13
Put on the whole amour of God, that ye may be able to stand against the wiles of the devil. For we wrestle not against flesh and blood, but against principalities, against powers, against the rulers of the darkness of this world, against spiritual wickedness in high places. Wherefore take unto you the whole amour of God, that ye may be able to withstand in the evil day, and having done all, to stand.

The Book of Colossians

Colossians 1:13
Who hath delivered us from the power of darkness, and hath translated us into the kingdom of his dear Son:

Colossians 2:15
And having spoiled principalities and powers, he made a shew of them openly, triumphing over them in it.

The Book of 2 Thessalonians

2 Thessalonians 3:2
And that **we may be delivered from unreasonable and wicked men:** for all men have not faith.

The Books of 1 & 2 Timothy

1 Timothy 3:6
Not a novice, lest being **lifted up with pride he fall into the condemnation of the devil.**

1 Timothy 3:7
Moreover he must have a good report of them which are without; **lest he fall into reproach and the snare of the devil.**

1 Timothy 4:1
Now the Spirit speaketh expressly, that in the latter times some shall depart from the faith, **giving heed to seducing spirits, and doctrines of devils;**

1 Timothy 5:15
For some are already turned aside after Satan.

2 Timothy 2:26
And that they may recover themselves out of the snare of the devil, who are taken captive by him at his will.

2 Timothy 4:17
Notwithstanding the Lord stood with me, and strengthened me; that by me the preaching might be fully known, and that all the Gentiles might hear: **and I was delivered out of the mouth of the lion.**

The Book of Hebrews

Hebrews 2:14
Forasmuch then as the children are partakers of flesh and blood, he also himself likewise took part of the same; **that through death he might destroy him that had the power of death, that is, the devil;**

Hebrews 2:15
And **deliver them who through fear of death were all their lifetime subject to bondage.**

Hebrews 11:29
By faith they passed through the Red sea as by dry land: which the Egyptians assaying to do were drowned.

Hebrews 12:13
And make straight paths for your feet, lest that which is lame be turned out of the way; but let it rather be healed.

Hebrews 13:6
So that we may boldly say, **The Lord is my helper, and I will not fear what man shall do unto me.**

The Book of James

James 2:19
Thou believest that there is one God; thou doest well: **the devils also believe, and tremble.**

James 3:15
This wisdom descendeth not from above, but is earthly, sensual, **devilish.**

James 3:16
For where envying and strife is, there is confusion and every evil work.

James 4:7
Submit yourselves therefore to God. Resist the devil, and he will flee from you.

James 5:16
Confess your faults one to another, and pray one for another, that ye may be healed. **The effectual fervent prayer of a righteous man availeth much.**

The Books of 1 & 2 Peter

1 Peter 5:8-9
Be sober, be vigilant; because your adversary the devil, as a roaring lion, walketh about, seeking whom he may devour: Whom resist stedfast in the faith, knowing that the same afflictions are accomplished in your brethren that are in the world.

2 Peter 2:7
And delivered just Lot, vexed with the filthy conversation of the wicked:

2 Peter 2:9
The Lord knoweth how to deliver the godly out of temptations, and to reserve the unjust unto the day of judgment to be punished:

The Book of 1 John

1 John 3:8
He that committeth sin is of the devil; for the devil sinneth from the beginning. For this purpose the Son of God was manifested, that he might destroy the works of the devil.

1 John 3:10
In this the children of God are manifest, and the children of the devil: whosoever doeth not righteousness is not of God, neither he that loveth not his brother.

1 John 4:18
There is no fear in love; but perfect love casteth out fear: **because fear hath torment. He that feareth is not made perfect in love.**

The Book of Revelation

Revelation 1:5
And from Jesus Christ, who is the faithful witness, and the first begotten of the dead, and the prince of the kings of the earth. Unto him that loved us, and washed us from our sins in his own blood,

Revelation 2:7

...**To him that overcometh** will I give to eat of the Tree of Life, which is in the midst of the paradise of God.

Revelation 2:8

...**He that overcometh** shall not be hurt of the second death.

Revelation 2:17

...**To him that overcometh** will I give to eat of the hidden manna, and will give him a white stone, and in the stone a new name written, which no man knoweth saving he that receiveth it.

Revelation 2:26

And he that overcometh, and keepeth my works unto the end, to him will I give power over the nations: And he shall rule them with a rod of iron; as vessels of a potter shall they be broken shivers: even as I received of my Father. And I will give him the morning star.

Revelation 3:5

He that overcometh, the same shall be clothed in white raiment; and I will not blot out his name out of the Book of Life, but I will confess his name before my Father, and before the angels.

Revelation 3:12
Him that overcometh will I make a pillar in the Temple of my God, and he shall go no more out: and I will write upon him the name of my God, which is new Jerusalem, which cometh down out of heaven from my God: and I will write upon him My new name.

Revelation 12:11
And they overcame him by the blood of the Lamb, and by the word of their testimony; and they loved not their lives unto the death.

Revelation 16:14
For they are the spirits of devils, working miracles, which go forth unto the kings of the earth and of the whole world, to gather them to the battle of that great day of God Almighty.

Revelation 17: 14
These shall make war with Lamb, and the Lamb shall overcome them: For he is the Lord of lords, and the King of kings: and they that are with Him are called, and chosen, and faithful.

Revelation 18:2
And he cried mightily with a strong voice, saying, **Babylon the great is fallen, is fallen, and is become the habitation of devils, and the hold of every foul spirit, and a cage of every unclean and hateful bird.**

Revelation 18:4
And I heard another voice from heaven, saying, **Come out of her, my people, that ye be not partakers of her sins, and that ye receive not of her plagues.**

Revelation 19:13
And he was clothed with a vesture dipped in blood: and his name is called The Word of God.

Revelation 20:9 & 10
...And fire came down from God out of heaven, and devoured them. And the devil that deceived them was cast into the lake of fire and brimstone, where the beast, and the false prophet are, and shall be tormented day and night for ever and ever.

Revelation 22:2
In the midst of the street of it, and on either side of the river, was there the tree of life, which bare

twelve manner of fruits, and yielded her fruit every month: **and the leaves of the tree were for the healing of the nations.**

ABOUT THE AUTHOR

JOHN ECKHARDT is overseer of Crusaders Ministries, located in Chicago, Illinois. Anointed with a strong apostolic grace, he has ministered throughout the United States and overseas in more than eighty nations. He is founder and overseer of the Impact Network, a sought-after international conference speaker, and has authored more than forty books including Prayers That Rout Demons, God Still Speaks and Prophet Arise. He resides in the Chicago area with his wife, Wanda, their five children and son in law.

FOR MORE INFORMATION

www.johneckhardtministries.com

14715372R00060

Printed in Great Britain
by Amazon.co.uk, Ltd.,
Marston Gate.